Properties of Matter

Aaron Carr and Lesley Evans Ogden

www.av2books.com

AV² provides enriched content that supplements and complements this book. Weigl's AV² books strive to create inspired learning and engage young minds in a total learning experience.

Your AV² Media Enhanced books come alive with...

Go to **www.av2books.com**, and enter this book's unique code.

BOOK CODE

P926072

AV² by Weigl brings you media enhanced books that support active learning.

Audio
Listen to sections of the book read aloud.

Video
Watch informative video clips.

Embedded Weblinks
Gain additional information for research.

Try This!
Complete activities and hands-on experiments.

Key Words
Study vocabulary, and complete a matching word activity.

Quizzes
Test your knowledge.

Slide Show
View images and captions, and prepare a presentation.

... and much, much more!

Published by AV² by Weigl
350 5th Avenue, 59th Floor
New York, NY 10118
Website: www.av2books.com   www.weigl.com

Library of Congress Cataloging-in-Publication Data

Evans Ogden, Lesley J. (Lesley Joan), 1968-
 Properties of matter / Lesley Evans Ogden.
   p. cm. -- (Physical science)
Includes bibliographical references and index.
ISBN 978-1-61690-730-3 (hardcover : alk. paper) -- ISBN 978-1-61690-734-1 (softcover : alk. paper)
1. Matter--Properties--Juvenile literature. I. Title.
QC173.16.E93 2012
530.4--dc22
                        2011002296

Printed in the United States of America in North Mankato, Minnesota
1 2 3 4 5 6 7 8 9 0 15 14 13 12 11

052011
WEP37500

Project Coordinator Aaron Carr
Design Terry Paulhus

CONTENTS

Water is the only common form of **matter** that exists in Earth's environment in the form of a solid, as ice or snow, a liquid, as water, and a gas, as steam. Water is made up of two hydrogen **atoms** and one oxygen atom. This is represented as H_2O. Water can change from a liquid to a solid to a gas, but its chemical makeup of H_2O stays the same.

Studying the Properties of Matter

Everything people can see and touch around them is an example of matter. The study of matter and its **properties** is covered by the branches of science known as **chemistry** and **physics**.

Matter exists in different states depending on temperature. The three states of matter most often observed are solids, liquids, and gases. Matter can change from one state to another when the temperature is raised or lowered. Different forms of matter change states at different temperatures. Most forms of matter are solids when cold, liquids when warm, and gases when hot.

■ A thermometer can be used to measure temperature. As the temperature rises, the liquid in the thermometer expands to fill up more of the glass tube.

Physical and Chemical Properties

All properties of matter are either extensive or intensive properties. An extensive property is one that cannot be used to determine the type of matter on its own. This includes properties such as **mass**, **volume**, and shape. An intensive property is unique to the type of matter. **Density** is an intensive property that can be used to help identify matter. Water, for example, can come in any mass or volume, but its density at a given temperature is always the same. Other intensive properties include color and **solubility**.

■ Scientists often measure many extensive properties to identify a type of matter.

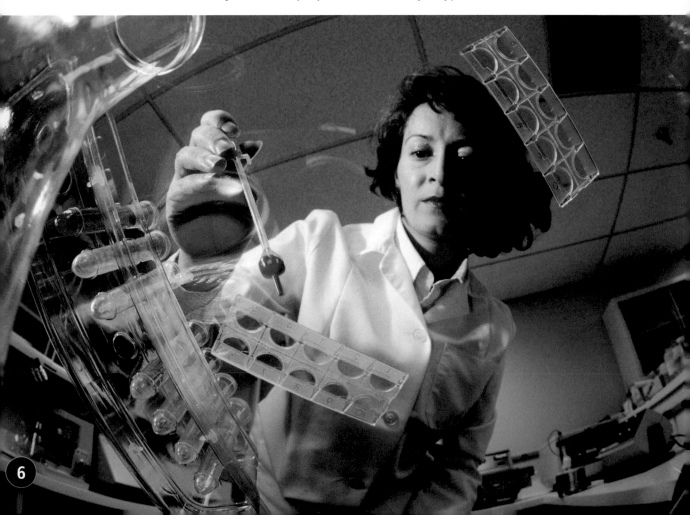

6

Measuring extensive properties can help determine intensive properties. To determine what type of liquid is contained in a sample, a scientist may first measure its volume and mass. Knowing these two extensive properties, the scientist can then calculate the density. This is done by dividing the mass by the volume. Once the intensive property of density is known, the scientist will have a better idea of what the liquid is.

CHEMICAL AND PHYSICAL CHANGES

All types of matter can change in one of two ways. Physical changes affect extensive properties. This means these changes do not change the type of matter. Chemical changes affect intensive properties. This means a chemical change results in a new type of matter being formed. Physical changes can be reversed, but chemical changes are often permanent. For example, freezing water to form ice or adding sugar to water are physical changes. Both of these changes can be easily reversed. Adding an oxygen atom to water, however, would result in a new chemical, hydrogen peroxide.

■ Bunsen burners are often used in labs to perform chemical changes.

Elements and Compounds

All matter is made of atoms. Atoms can group together to form **molecules**. If the atoms of the molecule are the same type, the molecule is an element. If the atoms are different from one another, the molecule is called a compound.

Elements can be made of one or more atoms. The atoms in an element are always the same. Elements cannot be broken down into simpler types of matter. For example, oxygen is an element. However, oxygen can also be a molecule. Two oxygen atoms join together to form an oxygen molecule. This is represented as O_2.

THE PERIODIC TABLE OF THE ELEMENTS

The periodic table lists all known elements. It also shows information about the properties of each element. Each of the known elements is numbered from 1 to 103. The elements are also given a one- or two-letter symbol that represents the element. For example, carbon is represented by the letter 'C', while the letters 'Au' stand for the element gold.

The elements are arranged into groups, periods, and colored blocks. Each column in the table is a group, and each row is a period. Each set of elements with the same colored squares are part of a block. Elements in the same period, group, or block share many of the same properties.

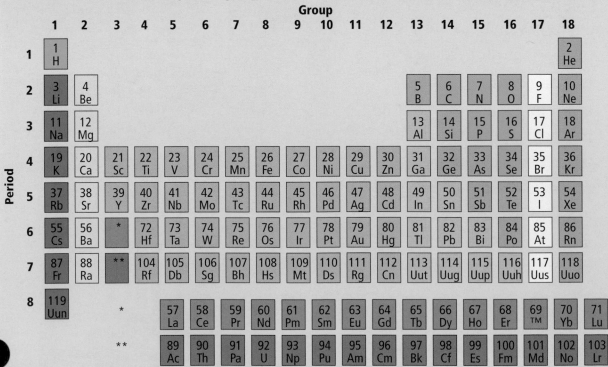

Compounds consist of two or more different atoms that are joined. Through chemical reactions, compounds can be broken down into simpler types of matter. Compounds display different properties than the elements or molecules that make them up. An example of a compound is carbon dioxide. Carbon dioxide, or CO_2, is made of two oxygen atoms joined to a carbon atom.

ELEMENTS

- Elements are specific kinds of atoms.
- They serve as the foundation for all forms of matter.
- Elements include hydrogen, H, nitrogen, N, and carbon, C.

MOLECULES

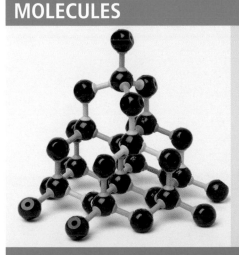

- Molecules contain two or more atoms of the same kind that are joined together.
- Some molecules are elements.
- Molecules include hydrogen, H_2, and nitrogen, N_2.

COMPOUNDS

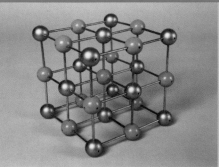

- Compounds are made of two or more different kinds of elements joined together.
- All compounds are molecules, but not all molecules are compounds.
- Compounds include water, H_2O, and salt, NaCl. Salt is the result of sodium, Na, and chlorine, Cl, atoms joining together.

Solutions and Mixtures

Mixtures and solutions are created when two or more different elements or compounds are combined through a physical change. Mixtures can be broken down into the parts that make them up through another physical change. For example, adding sand to a jar of water and stirring will create a mixture of sand and water. This physical change can be reversed by filtering the sand out of the water. Mixtures often have the same physical properties as the parts they are made from. The key characteristic of a mixture is that it does not appear to be a pure substance. The parts that make up a mixture are visible. In other words, it is **heterogeneous**.

A solution is a mixture that is **homogeneous**. This means all of the parts of the solution are evenly spread out. For example, if sugar were used instead of sand in the previous example, the result would be a solution of sugar water. This is because, when the sugar is stirred into the water, the sugar dissolves. This creates a solution with the sugar evenly spread throughout the water.

■ Combining two substances is not often enough to create a solution. Stirring, heating, or some other action is usually needed for a solution to form.

A solution is the result of a physical change. This means the parts of a solution can be separated by another physical change. In the example, the sugar water solution can be reversed by heating the water until it boils away, leaving the sugar behind.

The simplest solution is made by combining a **solute** with a **solvent**. A solute is the substance that will be dissolved, and the solvent is the substance that will do the dissolving. In the above example, sugar is the solute, and water is the solvent.

HOMOGENEOUS

- A homogeneous substance is thought to be a pure solution.

- Solutions appear to be a single substance when seen without the aid of a microscope.

- All parts of a solution are spread out evenly. This means both the solute and the solvent appear to be one liquid.

HETEROGENEOUS

- A heterogeneous substance is thought to be a mixture.

- Mixtures appear to have several parts that make them up, even when viewed without the aid of a microscope.

- The parts that make up a mixture are not spread out evenly. This means the solute is visible in the solvent.

Properties of Matter Discoveries Around the World

ARCTIC OCEAN

NORTH AMERICA

PACIFIC OCEAN

ATLANTIC OCEAN

SOUTH AMERICA

Year: 1879
Location: Great Britain
Fast Fact: English physicist Sir William Crookes discovered a fourth state of matter. This state is later called plasma. Plasma is similar to a gas but is strongly affected by electricity. Plasmas are now known to be the most common state of matter. Plasmas account for an estimated 99 percent of the observable universe.

Year: 1964
Location: United States
American physicists Murray Gell-Mann and George Zweig proposed that a particle smaller than an atom exists. These particles, which are called quarks, are now thought to be "elementary particles." Elementary particles cannot be broken down into anything smaller.

LEGEND

★ FEATURED DISCOVERIES

N
W E
S

SCALE
621 Miles
0   1,000 Kilometers

WHAT HAVE YOU LEARNED ABOUT DISCOVERIES?

This map shows the locations of some of the major scientific discoveries that have occurred around the world. Use this map, and research online to answer these questions.

1. Which continent has had the most discoveries about the properties of matter?
2. How were most of these discoveries made?

ARCTIC OCEAN

EUROPE

AFRICA

Year: 1924–1925
Location: India and Germany
Fast Fact: Indian physicist Satyendra Nath Bose and Albert Einstein proposed a fifth state of matter. It took 70 years for scientists to prove Bose and Einstein right. This state is often called a superfluid. A superfluid can only form at extremely low temperatures. One of the best-known superfluids is a type of helium that is cooled to a temperature of −456° Fahrenheit (−271° Celsius).

PACIFIC OCEAN

AUSTRALIA

INDIAN OCEAN

Year: 1910
Location: New Zealand
Fast Fact: After the discovery of the **electron** a few years earlier, physicist Ernest Rutherford set out to test the inner workings of the atom. He designed an experiment that should have had predictable results. The results, however, could not have been further from his predictions. This led Rutherford to propose that atoms are made up of electrons circling a **nucleus**. This was the first model of the atom to propose that atoms contain a central nucleus.

ANTARCTICA

Changing States

All elements and compounds can change from one state to another through a physical change. This change often requires a change in temperature. Generally, elements will become solids at cold temperatures, liquids at mid-range temperatures, and gases at hot temperatures.

The molecule oxygen, O_2, is a gas at room temperature. When oxygen is cooled to very low temperatures, it will first become a liquid and then a solid. As a liquid and solid, the oxygen atoms that make up the molecules remain the same, O_2. All that changes is how densely, or tightly, the oxygen molecules pack together. As a gas, the molecules are spaced far apart. As a solid, the molecules are packed together tightly.

■ Nitrogen becomes a liquid at −321°F (−196°C). Liquid nitrogen is so cold that placing most objects into it will cause them to freeze instantly. Objects frozen in this way break easily.

MOVING MOLECULES

The state of matter refers to how fast molecules are moving. In a solid, molecules are attached to each other. The molecules in a solid vibrate in place a little bit, but they do not move around much. In a liquid, molecules are held together more loosely. The molecules of a liquid move around, but they stay fairly close together. In a gas, the molecules move around much more and spread far apart from one another.

Each of these states of matter is also called a phase. States, or phases, change from one to another if energy is added or taken away. The state of matter can change when the temperature changes. Generally, as the temperature rises, matter moves to a more active state. Solid is the least active state, while gas is the most active.

The points at which states change are called the **melting point** and the **boiling point**. When a liquid heats up to its boiling point and forms a gas, the process is called evaporation. The opposite happens when the temperature falls. The molecules in the substance slow down, and gas changes into a liquid. This process is called condensation. As molecules in a liquid cool, they reach their **freezing point** and turn into a solid.

Some substances can go from solid to gas without first becoming a liquid. This process is called sublimation. The opposite process, from gas to solid, is called deposition. A common substance that can sublimate is carbon dioxide. Solid carbon dioxide is called dry ice. Dry ice sublimates to form a foggy gas. For this reason, dry ice is often used in fog machines.

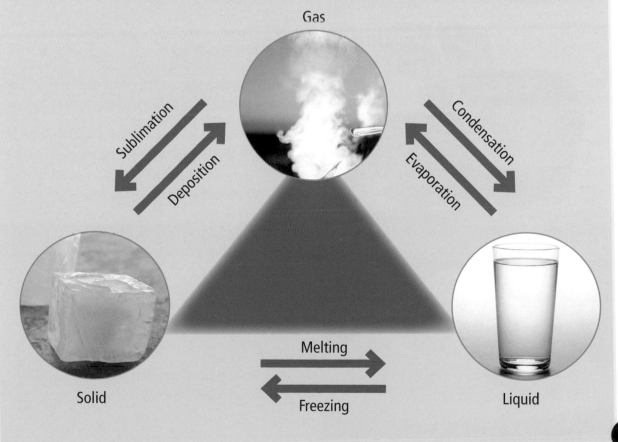

Gas

Sublimation

Deposition

Condensation

Evaporation

Melting

Freezing

Solid

Liquid

States of Matter

In addition to the three main states of matter—solid, liquid, and gas—there are two other known states of matter. These two states are plasma and superfluid. Plasmas are common throughout the universe, but they are more rare on Earth.

GASES

- Gases have no definite volume or shape.
- They are weakly affected by electric or **magnetic fields**.
- If a gas is put into a container, it will expand to fill the space.

LIQUIDS

- Liquids have a definite volume but no definite shape.
- They are able to flow, but they are affected by the force of **friction**.
- If a liquid is poured from one container to another, it will take on the shape of the new container. However, the volume of the liquid will stay the same.

SOLIDS

- Solids have a definite volume and shape.
- They are quite rigid, tending to stay the same size and shape.
- A solid does not flow to fill the container it is placed in.

Superfluids were first produced in a lab in 1995. They only exist at very low temperatures, close to **absolute zero**. Some scientists now believe there may be a sixth state of matter. This state is called a supersolid. The existence of supersolids has not yet been proven.

PLASMAS

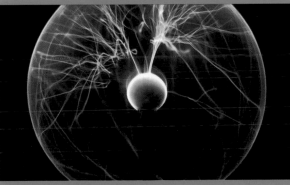

- Plasmas are similar to gases but contain electric **charges**.

- They are strongly affected by electricity and magnetic fields.

SUPERFLUIDS

- Superfluids resemble a normal liquid.

- They are able to flow without being affected by forces of friction.

- Superfluids can flow upward. If a bucket is placed into a pool of superfluid, the superfluid will flow up the sides of the bucket and begin filling the bucket on its own. It will not stop until the level of the superfluid is the same both inside and outside of the bucket.

SUPERSOLIDS

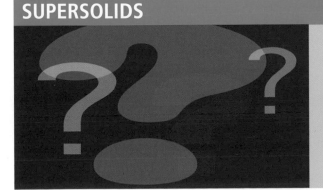

- Supersolids have not yet been proven to exist.

- They are predicted to have similar properties to a superfluid.

- Scientists predict a supersolid would be both solid and able to flow, like a liquid.

Properties of Matter Timeline

475 BC — 1600 AD — 1700 — 1800 — 1869 — 1897 — 1900 — 1910 — 1920 — 1930 — 1940 — 1995

1 **2** **3** **4** **5** **6** **7** **8** **9** **10** **11** **13**

12

1 **475 BC**
Leucippus is the first to propose that all matter is made up of atoms.

2 **1600s AD**
Blaise Pascal shows that pressure applied to one point of a liquid is transmitted unchanged to all points in the liquid.

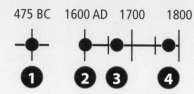

3 **1662**
Robert Boyle shows that, if a fixed amount of gas is kept at a constant temperature, the volume will decrease as the pressure is increased.

4 **1787**
Jacques-Alexandre Charles discovers the relationship between temperature and the change in volume of a gas.

5 **1869**
Dmitri Mendeleev creates the periodic table of elements.

6 **1897**
The electron is discovered by British researcher Joseph John Thomson.

7 **1905**
Albert Einstein shows that mass and energy are related.

8 **1913**
Niels Bohr proposes his theory of atomic structure.

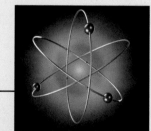

9 **1924**
Louis de Broglie proposes that particles of matter behave like waves.

10 **1932**
James Chadwick identifies the neutron. Then, Werner Heisenberg proposes the nucleus of an atom consists of protons and neutrons.

11 **1933**
Swiss astronomer Fritz Zwicky proposes that there must be more matter in the universe than can be seen. The "missing" matter is called dark matter.

12 **1933**
German engineer Ernst Ruska invents the electron microscope. This allows scientists to better study atoms and other small particles.

13 **1995**
American scientists Carl Wieman and Eric Cornell prove the existence of superfluids, a fifth state of matter.

What is a Chemist?

A chemist is a person that studies chemistry. Chemistry is the science of matter and its properties. Chemists study what happens when different types of matter are heated, cooled, or mixed. They study atoms and molecules. Chemists may work at universities, factories, environmental labs, water treatment plants, or many other places.

Many chemists invent new products or new technologies. They have created items such as gas masks for firefighters, new drugs to fight disease, batteries, and new types of energy that are better for the environment. Many chemists try to create new materials that can be used in everyday products. Some chemists might create stronger plastics, while others work on clothing fabrics that do not wrinkle or stain.

Niels Bohr

Niels Bohr (1885–1962) was a Danish scientist best known for his work on the structure of atoms. In 1913, he proposed a new theory of atomic structure. Bohr's model of the atom suggested that electrons travel in different levels around the nucleus. Bohr was awarded the Nobel Prize in 1922 for his work on atomic structure.

EDUCATION

Most chemists have a master's degree or a doctoral degree in chemistry. People interested in becoming a chemist should take advanced courses in math and science.

WORKING CONDITIONS

Chemists often work in laboratories. They usually work as part of a team with other chemists and people from different educational backgrounds, such as engineers and computer scientists.

Six Facts About the Properties of Matter

Diamonds, a pure form of carbon, are the hardest natural material found on Earth.

Nitrogen is a chemical that is usually found as a gas. To become a liquid, nitrogen gas must be cooled to about −321°F (−196°C).

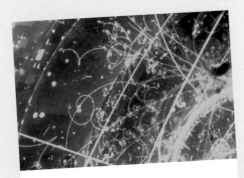

A tiny particle called a muon was discovered in 1936. The muon is similar to an electron but is 207 times heavier.

Plants take in carbon dioxide through their leaves. Through a process called photosynthesis, they use the carbon dioxide to produce sugars that they need to grow.

The molecules in a liquid stick together through forces called cohesion.

Liquids are difficult, if not impossible, to squeeze into a smaller volume.

Properties of Matter
Brain Teasers

1 What state of matter has a definite volume but not a definite shape?

2 In which state of matter are the molecules packed together the most?

3 What is the name of the force that holds molecules in a liquid together?

4 What is the name of the process that occurs when a solid changes to gas without first becoming a liquid?

5 What is the most common state of matter that occurs in the universe?

6 What is the hardest solid found in nature?

7 Is water a molecule or a compound?

8 When a liquid is heated and becomes a gas, what is this change called?

9 What is a liquid called when it appears to be a single, pure substance?

10 What type of change occurs when a substance is burned?

Science in Action

See Your Breath

What causes bathroom mirrors to steam up after a hot shower? The answer is water vapor, the gas form of water. In this experiment, you will see water vapor change from an invisible gas to tiny liquid droplets.

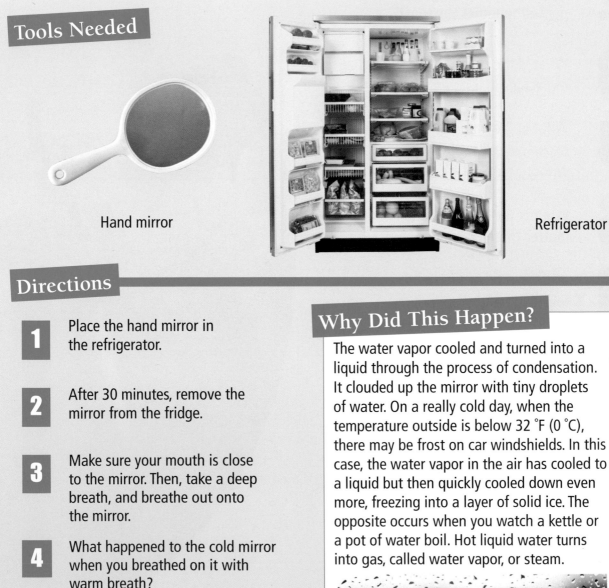

Hand mirror

Refrigerator

Directions

1 Place the hand mirror in the refrigerator.

2 After 30 minutes, remove the mirror from the fridge.

3 Make sure your mouth is close to the mirror. Then, take a deep breath, and breathe out onto the mirror.

4 What happened to the cold mirror when you breathed on it with warm breath?

Why Did This Happen?

The water vapor cooled and turned into a liquid through the process of condensation. It clouded up the mirror with tiny droplets of water. On a really cold day, when the temperature outside is below 32 °F (0 °C), there may be frost on car windshields. In this case, the water vapor in the air has cooled to a liquid but then quickly cooled down even more, freezing into a layer of solid ice. The opposite occurs when you watch a kettle or a pot of water boil. Hot liquid water turns into gas, called water vapor, or steam.

Words to Know

absolute zero: the coldest possible temperature; −459.76°F (−273.15°C)

atoms: the basic units of matter

boiling point: the temperature at which matter changes from liquid to gas

charges: properties of matter responsible for electricity; can be either positive or negative

chemistry: the science of matter and its properties

density: a measure of how tightly or loosely packed the elements of a molecule or compound are

electrons: particles with a negative charge that circle the nucleus of an atom

freezing point: the point at which molecules in a liquid cool down and turn into a solid

friction: a force created when two surfaces rub together

heterogeneous: a mixture that displays different parts

homogeneous: a solution that appears as a single, or pure, substance

magnetic fields: areas that are affected by magnetic forces

mass: a measure of the amount of matter in an object; related to weight

matter: anything that has mass and takes up space

melting point: the temperature at which matter goes from solid to liquid

molecules: two or more atoms joined together

nucleus: the center of an atom; contains particles with positive and neutral charges

physics: the study of matter and energy

properties: characteristics, or traits, of a substance

solubility: ability to be dissolved in a liquid

solute: the minor part of a solution that is dissolved into the solution

solvent: the major part of a solution that dissolves a solute

volume: the amount of space taken up by an object

Index

Log on to www.av2books.com

AV² by Weigl brings you media enhanced books that support active learning. Go to www.av2books.com, and enter the special code found on page 2 of this book. You will gain access to enriched and enhanced content that supplements and complements this book. Content includes video, audio, web links, quizzes, a slide show, and activities.

Audio
Listen to sections of the book read aloud.

Video
Watch informative video clips.

Embedded Weblinks
Gain additional information for research.

Try This!
Complete activities and hands-on experiments.

WHAT'S ONLINE?

 Try This!	Embedded Weblinks	Video	EXTRA FEATURES
Test your knowledge about types of matter.	Read a quick review of the basics of matter.	Watch a video introduction to the properties of matter.	**Audio** Listen to sections of the book read aloud.
Identify the states of matter.	Access more information about specific topics in matter.	Watch another video about the properties of matter.	**Key Words** Study vocabulary, and complete a matching word activity.
Add your own facts to the fact section.	Explore interactive learning tools.		
Find out more about the properties of matter through an educational activity.	Find out more about the different states of matter.		**Slide Show** View images and captions, and prepare a presentation.
	Learn more about the history of researching properties of matter.		
	Read about an important scientist.		**Quizzes** Test your knowledge.

AV² was built to bridge the gap between print and digital. We encourage you to tell us what you like and what you want to see in the future.

Sign up to be an AV² Ambassador at www.av2books.com/ambassador.